Born in Burntwood

Born in Burntwood

DIANE PARKER

Copyright © 2018 by Diane Parker.

ISBN:	Softcover	978-1-5434-9252-1
	eBook	978-1-5434-9251-4

All rights reserved. No part of this book may be reproduced or transmitted in any form or by any means, electronic or mechanical, including photocopying, recording, or by any information storage and retrieval system, without permission in writing from the copyright owner.

Any people depicted in stock imagery provided by Getty Images are models, and such images are being used for illustrative purposes only.
Certain stock imagery © Getty Images.

Print information available on the last page.

Rev. date: 09/11/2018

To order additional copies of this book, contact:
Xlibris
800-056-3182
www.Xlibrispublishing.co.uk
Orders@Xlibrispublishing.co.uk
784736

Contents

The Biscuit under the chair 1
Cruising Days 2
Butterfly 3
Ain't no Pam Aires 4
Cycle Ride 5
Hair in style 6
Forget 8
In the barracks 9
Hometown Hues 10
Unconventional 12
Hurt 13
Checkouts chant 15
Cruising Days 16
Starry Night 17
Cycle Ride 18
Rain 19
Secure 21
Words 22
Butterfly 23
Teachers 24
So star trek 26
In the garden (2) 27
Football crazy 29
The drug 31
Seasons 33
Namely Names 34
On Common Ground 35
The Pitts 36
The Help 37
On line 38
Triangle memories 39

I cannot express enough thanks to Ian Atkins
for his continued support and assistance
during the publishing of this book

The Biscuit under the chair

There's a biscuit there under the chair and sit n plead I stop and stare

What are u doing get over there I flash a frown and send a glare

Don't know why I bother to spit n sniff and slobber

They hardly look don't think they care just send me here
and over there and so continue to do their stuff the nuisance
dog that howling mutt my best paws I even put

So I'll continue to to stink n smelly in hope they will
forget the telly and give me that meat well hid from the
del if I give the sad old eyes looks some Welly

I may just may get treated fair and get my
biscuit from under the chair

Cruising Days

Carefree cruising days ahead away from the dire n dank n dread

A chariot vessel to take us far no hustle n bustle who needs a car

For we have the waterways to explore while
others are stuck in traffic what chore

Must get shipshape first it's true lots for us to plan and do

First put right what needs to be done then it's good and then it's fun

Stumble and bumble our way through locks
in 6months may find docks

Cooling water Keeps us afloat got our vessel find our moute

Starting engine setting off till were at our mooring spot

Butterfly

Butterfly oh wings expanding swift in height and grace in landing
butterfly oh what fun flying in the summer sun

How I wish could take a flight and see what u see in all its might

Would go here would go there where to go to wouldn't care

Carefree days and cool fresh nights all
those sounds and all those sights

Take me with u let's just see let's just go just u and me

Ain't no Pam Aires

Ain't no Pam Aires but love to write poems don't
know where it leads or where it is going

Just love the ryming words fantastic hold on to my hat
and my knicker elastic trying my thoughts down first
on paper hoping a wee bit of change I'll a maker

My pen is a running with thoughts that are flowing
while all that surround are out doing their mowing

With visions my name up in lights would be lovely
crack open the bottle a nice bit of bubbly

Maybe she'll notice and may take a glance will
never know unless take a chance

Relax with my poems a good way to chill
better than stressing or popping a pill

Can't think of no more so it's best that I close
time for a catnap or maybe a doze

Cycle Ride

As I cycle through the lanes today and
ponder in thought along the way

Past bush and bramble I scurry n scramble past
those that cycle and those that ramble

With cars that rush past for those in a dash worried they'll arrive
a bit late and may have to make their time up in lunch break

Past tractors in fields a ploughing away constantly
whirring and making their hay

Hair in style

Salon secrets shampoo n set running round with that hairnet

In they come n want it done going out n having fun

On our feet sweeping up washing all the coffee cups

Mixing colour pull through cap showing pictures on their app

Wedding hair it takes some planning
Blushing brides can be demanding
Know it's stress and will calm down
Gasps from all in salon abound
Looks so lovely all agreed
Came to rescue times in need

Time to trim n back to school
Spent all summer in the pool

Sort out change so sit on stool
Wrap up warm it's gone so cool

Time for taxi on its way
Steady clients through the day
Cash in drawers n tills a ringing
Coming back n lunch a bringing

Plod on through the afternoon
Hopefully will be done soon
Used to being on our feet
Swivel round on clients feet
All good children deserve a sweet

Locking up were all secure
Time to give the roads a tour
Key in door am home yip eey
Coffee food and what's to see

Forget

Don't know what I came here for
sure it's twice been through that door

Put in oven while baking on Monday
only to find still in there Sunday
when took a look can't find that book
I'm sure gone with elves when in they snook

And glasses please don't mention those
Had them on when took a doze
vanished now and not a trace looked in this and other space
better find them quick make haste must of put them safe some place

Bermuda triangle it must be
now be late for doing tea
think must stick it all with glue
will put a stop to huff and phew

Found them oh rejoice at last
stressful moment thence surpassed
so can carry on as norm
till next in Bermuda's storm

In the barracks

A hot summer evening
dreams flood head of leaving
This place for now I call home
The barracks the planes and the god awful drone

The siren wails it's time to scramble
no time to pace no time to amble

I fill with dread what lies ahead
In plane I go stiff upper lip tally ho
onwards to bear and onwards to go
Feelings of fear n dread my stomach
churns with visions I have in my head
The whir of the engine the panels aglow
no time to evact no time to say no

Formation abating were now on our way
This is our mission and this is our day
To attack the Luftwaffer and send them away
Guns are now silent time to go home
Head back to base now no more I'm alone
Out of the mission and out of the zone

On to debriefing all is unknown
Thoughts turn to wife thoughts turn to home

Missing her greatly missing her much
Words wrote in letters keeping in touch

Hometown Hues

My hometown means much to me
miners working roots are we
first church to have electricity
the wakes each year to watch and see

And To embark for smallest park
and spread the word across the world
in Stevens pride keep hope alive
beat cancers curse and to survive

Were playing children day and night
the Redwood slide were out of sight

Chase water splashing money cashing
out the waterfall are dashing

With common ground and dens abound
knock door run to runaround

The pubs and clubs we all frequented
boogies nights were heaven scented

Over brook n down the lanes
how we loved our well packed days

weekend scramble quarrys ensemble
clouds of dust n tyres screeching
blackberry bush I tried a reaching

Gone to fast our hometown past
from school days last to scholars blast
my home my special place to be
and would be same if you were me

Unconventional

Unconventional are we follow sheep
oh no not me
What we do n what's to be helps the air of mystery

All that's different and unique
brave and bold mild and meek
all we find and all we seek
Takes us through week by week

Hurt

After
years it's not right
Sting like a bee and cuts like a knife
Saw her message flash on screen
Now I know where u have been

Must admit I got it wrong
U have been here all along
Work obsessed was at my desk
As u know would never rest
She was there when thought lost care
Time together being so rare
Welcomed u with open arms keep u safe her special charms
Never knew how hurt would harm

Turned so distant
That's so true
Left me hurt and feeling blue

Now all I do each day is cry
Put on face and getting by
Can't think why u had to lie
All is past and time to fly

Cannot face our last good bye
Ends in sight and all is nigh
So u pack away Ur stuff
Why's it feel so very tough

Wish you well
With hope i tell
My fate is sealed
So that's the deal

So I watch u out the door
Stuffs all packed
So we're no more

Only hope ull think one day
And realise what's thrown away
Listen to what I have to say
Wait for that while down I lay

But for now it's silence here
Memories in heart
Which I find dear
Try to stifle back my tear
Oh turn back clock this time last year

Lets take stock it's not too late
Run to window still at gate
He's my heart my soul my mate
Without him life it just don't rate
Can't get back if hate don't abeit

Run on out I scream and shout
Turns on round more tears flood out
Drops his bags he's a crumbled mess
Guide him back it's time to rest

Gave my all and passed the test
Back home safe now I'm so blessed

Checkouts chant

Cashing up n checking out
So much hustle n bustle about
Trolleys filled so high it's reeling
Call security someone's stealing
Card to sign as someones leaving
Managers stressed and quietly seething

Try to think what's been forgot
Assure the customers in next lot
Time for lunch and something hot
Pens ran out give bin a shot

Keying products on the screen
Can you tell me wheres baked beans
Will u pack them bags are here
Ride on round and start to steer

Plants ore falling making mess
Smiling sweetly under duress
Sometimes have to take a guess
When try to help accept no less

Bells are ringing throughout store
Staff are running round for more
A bargains afoot and chickens galore
While supervisors feet are getting sore

Steady flow and coming through
Careful now and form a queue
Till last one is done and out
Smiling faces out we clock
Problems of the day now block

Cruising Days

Carefree cruising days ahead
away from the dire n dank n dread

A chariot vessel to take us far
no hustle n bustle who needs a car

For we have the waterways to explore
while others are stuck in traffic what chore

Must get shipshape first it's true
Lots for us to plan and do

First put right what needs to be done
Then it's good and then it's fun

Stumble and bumble our way through locks
In 6 months may find docks

Cooling water Keeps us afloat
Got our vessel find our mote

Starting engine setting off
Till were at our mooring spot

Starry Night

As I look up on a starry night
And marvel at all the wonderful delights
On an evening dark n crisp n clear
Hoot of an owl the only sound I hear
In the midnight black veneer
we are so far and yet so near
With thoughts turned to view that pinpoint of light
Deep in thought and deep in flight

Cycle Ride

As I cycle through the lanes today
And ponder in thought along the way

Past bush and bramble
I scurry n scramble past those that cycle and Those that ramble

With cars that rush past for those in a dash
worried they'll arrive a bit late
And may have to make their time up in lunch break

Past tractors in fields a ploughing away Constantly
whirring and making their hay

Rain

The cool fresh water seeping down
Thudding on pavements while hitting the ground
I look around there's not a sound
No sight of man or walking hound

So inside now we plan to stay
To keep the wet and cold away
With telly to watch and games to play
Were poised with treats n set for day

For those with pastimes it is good
That babies jacket needs a hood
And fill the air with baking smells
Will they last well time will tell

For those with energy to burn
That flat pack to focus study n learn
And hallway looks a little drab
A lick of paint n stencil pad
will cheer up that was looking sad

Quick lookout to the trees a swaying
Listen to whistling wind so eary
Inside it's all looking cheery
No time for doom n gloom and bleary

Work is done that's so much better
Sun's out now let's post that letter
Didn't moan it didn't matter
Whilst outside did belt and batter

Step on out avoid the puddles
Cleared n organised the muddles
A restful day from all the chaos
For whats achieved henceforth do say us
With weather done it's worse today
But we have had the last hooray

Secure

That happy place the special cure
Adorning all with our allure
Which makes us sure so very sure
When love lies in that open door where I will be For evermore

My strength enlight to know what's right
Achievement goals will stay in sight

It's very good it's very true
Taking form in claret n blue

To write within ur heart this said will never part Were growing older staying strong proving that we do belong

Peas in a pod we are chosen
He likes monsters I like frozen
Monsters are Inc but mainly in sinc
Are mostly alike got him on bike
And got me on hike with our ghostly encounters send scares overnight

Happiness good n happiness trends
Were now becoming really great friends
As well as in love we fit like a glove
A drink and a movie keeps us from pub

And when I've got my book in print
He is part of words that link
So complete can finally say
Take a look have a seat
writing Ur heartfelt words does pay

Words

Words of wisdom words of clout
Words can't Really do without
Words that thrill n words that Chill
Words that teach us meanings still
Words That are n words that be
Words for u n words for Me
Words are great u wait n see
Words that make Our history
Without words we' d all be stuck
That's The word n here's the book

Butterfly

Butterfly oh wings expanding swift in height and grace in landing
butterfly oh what fun flying in the summer sun

How I wish could take a flight and see what u see in all its might

Would go here would go there where to go to wouldn't care

Carefree days and cool fresh nights all
those sounds and all those sights

Take me with u let's just see let's just go just u and me

Teachers

Teachers work hard pens to push
Need to get through to morning rush
Wish my class could all just hush
While we all sort out this mush
To make and create our piece that's lush

Phew there goes the bell I think
Whose not washed their hands in sink
Exam works sent me on the brink
With need to sort that missing link

Bells gone like a herd they barge
Rise on up cause I'm in charge
Could eat a cowpat spread with Marg
So Mackie's after work be giving it large

So work on through to end of day
Another quick break and out to play
Rowdy noise outside hooray
What's been said and what to say
Afternoons pass so come what may

Bells gone great and out the gate
Soon on way n foods on wait
Quick. And easy on my plate
Time to rest and text my mate

That's much better hunger at bay
Home wood bound I'm on my way

Hence I come to this conclusion
Foundations mark our last solution
Too much work and too much pay
That is what they all do say
We all try and do our best
Homeward bound and time to rest

DIANE PARKER

So star trek

They make it so and boldly go
The clingons are approaching
And live in fear the Borg is near
Attack by romulins face severe

The crew and me do watch and see
Adventures across the galaxy

The neautral zone lies on timeline
Hail for frequencies sector nine

Transport at will can help them still
Next Gens favourite really brill
Old and new still love them do
With gamma quadrant course pursue

Years later going strong
Proving really does belong
Characters fans have grown to love
From early childhood look above

Science fiction fact run true
Powerful band of motley crew

When all's against situations dire
Kirk and Picard just won't retire
Transport warp speed Scotty now
Clingons bird of prey on bow

So settle down and programs run
Full speed ahead to sector one

In the garden (2)

In the gardens where I think of u
Chats to brother sky so blue
Putting all the world to rights
Watching all in natures sights

You always loved birds in Ur garden
Always one to find a bargain
Sent your meals back having puddings
Never knew be gone so sudden

Such a gentle nature by far
And a stubborn Taurean star
Dig Ur heels in if didn't want too
Hard work for a family l who loved you

Watched the soaps tell plot in Earnest
Your funny comments straight faced jest
Had us fall about with laughter
Such a pleasant memories capture

Gone to early that be true
Left us feeling sad and blue
Loved by family now expanded
As is known can be demanding

Always graced us with Ur knowledge
That at least has gave us solice
Your words of wisdom never fault ered
A faith in us which have never altered
Couldn't ask for any better
Write my thoughts down in a letter

Love of past I get from u
Carries through in family too
Love of film in black and white
Miss Ur talks and Ur in sights
So gain comfort in the view
Your in Ur garden sky so blue

Football crazy

Was 9 or ten
Wish was there that time again
Walking on up to the match
Got the football bug new batch

Through the turnstiles
And up the steps

Rows and rows of seats
As tension mounts
While all about
Are fans in executive suites

Some fans braving the cold
Shouting and being bold
Some young and some old
And on the pitch
The score is told

The players come out
And do their training
The weather has turned
And now it's raining

The game ends in another win
Set in stone and come on in
For Aston villa
What a thriller
My first ever game
The memories reign

Back home and tucked up in bed
Football, fans and songs through my head

Dozing off look at the program
Picture the fans in the stand that are loaden
Another quick peek
To do it next week

The pathway to glory
Tell history s story

The drug

Your the drug I need in life
Gives me hope and gives me strife
Without whom I'm feeling grim
Keeps me warm inside within

Insecure there is no cure
Gives my heart a guided tour
Sweet we are and will be too
Measured in the size of you
Love besottted through and through
Never ending ever true

We have been through lots together
It has torn our ropes to tether
But fight on as we will do
woo the day no time to rue
Gives the haters chance to coo

Heavens best your sweet suggest
Quick one liners said in jest
Good and true what can we do
Cannot go through da jar Vue

Won't give up am always yours
Watch u sleeping on my floors
Got to keep an eye on doors
On telly mighty lions roars

Seasons

Seasons come and seasons go
Summer sun and autumn glow
Spring has sprung
And not too long
Winters worst and Christmas Song
Family Freind's and all belong

The warmth on skin
And cold within
To teach us all are born in sin
From all around
Winds howling sound
And lead us on to snowy ground

So take a chair
With not a care
And watch the fireworks gentle flare
The signs of life
To so entice
Were over winters sacrifice

We do emplore
To buy some more
The summer clearance now in store
Let's go and see that winters tree
A sight behold for all with glee

Now we must reap
The years we keep
The celebrations we do seek
Will add all on to our mystique

DIANE PARKER

Namely Names

Boney Hay up Belgium way keeping Waterloo at bay
Then head on down to Burntwood Town
The forest burning all around
Hence Hamors Wic do take a pick
All of farmers dug out ditch

The names renound for sight and sound
All our waterfronts benound
Ye olde en times passed down this rymth
Give out a slow and steady vibe
Whence we are back in olden times

On Common Ground

Early morning the common beckons
Don't want to waste precious seconds

On our bikes and call on mates
Riding past houses and open gates

Off onto gentleshaw
Known as the common
The hours on here
Never be forgotton

Down to the brook
To build a damn
With bricks rocks and stones
That is our plan

Then off up the sand hills
Standing on the edge
We're kings of the common
We shout our pledge

Then run through all the ferns and Heather
Glorious day and lovely weather

End of the day and back home for tea
Will the damn still be standing
have to wait and see

DIANE PARKER

The Pitts

Chasetown is the Pitts u see
Mining town which grew to be
Formed by marquis of Anglesey

Water basins number one
Hauled it up and on the line
Work define them in the mine
Drawn December fires ember
All are working hard to render
Marquis was lining
coal chunks are flying
Profit in coal are not denying

200 tons in number two
Fly flew in and in she blew
Cathedral as known locally
Stoke the fire n time for tea
Closed down just as war was started
Men were marching out and parted

Closed it down in fifty six
Futures built in microchips
Quick and easy and more equipt
Deep below and dust is thick

The working mine were just so glorious
Even though the works laborius
They do the work and get the pay
And get through yet another day

The Help

Helping all that need the help
Clearing all those cupboards out
Open jars and bottles alike
Always went there on my bike

Freinddship made along the way
What will we need done today
Always greeted with a smile
Sometimes with hols had been a while

Always done my very best
Taken on had passed the test
Showing tenderness times of ill
Making sure have had their pill

Satisfaction for job well done
Giving strength to carry on
Sharing all our weekly news
Filling someone else's shoes

Glad I gave it all a go
Move around and going slow
Always sad when are no more
Thoughts to them when pass their door
Part of memories ever more
Chats and laughs so sweet and sure

For those who think may try it too
Please give a go the best you'd do

DIANE PARKER

On line

Internet hell I have to tell
It drives me mads frustrating
Password this and log in that
My work is done and waiting

Please email more
Tis such a chore
You can check websites websites galore
Trawling through endless ads is a bore
Gonna be here for evermore

Note attached file
Am in such a denial
Can sign take a trial
But may be a while
Cause just ain't my style

Calling up oh dear I'm stuck
Voice on phone it just don't listen
Try keep calm my blood pressures risen
Please call back cause lines are busy
Gets me in a proper tizzy
Reach for refreshing energy fizzy

Then rejoice it's worked and sent
Comes back red just wasn't meant
Tap in slowly watch each bit
Hours n hours I have to sit

Ask a friend they haven't time
Say its easy to do to do online
Forget it now and do it later
Kettle on and read the paper

Triangle memories

The triangle is where I grew up
Across the road and jump the brook
It was know as my first home
Across the cornfields I would roam

Up the farmers field on haystacks
Chased us down and run all way back
Long hot summer of 76
Hot pants Osmond's and building bricks
Building dens and play with Freind's
Never wanted it to end

Hush up now and tape top forty
Crackerjack and Jackanory
Cows in garden eating veges
Top of slope were on our sledges

Going up the road to shop
Off the licence got ice pops
Flashing lights across the green
Hoping that we wasn't seen

Whose the king of the castle would shout
Your the dirty rascal keep out
Taking pet to be looked after
Careful in loft just watch that rafter

Playing tig with our gang
Wombles theme we all did sang
Obstacles course spread all out back
Dominoes tower for me to stack

All too soon and all grown up
The heartfelt memories for my book

Printed in Great Britain
by Amazon